ORPHAN T
RIDER

Orphan Train Rider

One Boy's True Story

by Andrea Warren

Clarion Books
An Imprint of HarperCollins*Publishers*
Boston   New York

Manufactured in China

Book design by Sylvia Frezzolini Severance
The text of this book is set in 13.5-point Bembo.

22 SCP 35 34 33 32 31 30 29

Library of Congress Cataloging-in-Publication Data

Warren, Andrea.
Orphan train rider: one boy's true story / by Andrea Warren.
p. cm.
Summary: Discusses the placement of over 200,000 orphaned or abandoned children
in homes throughout the Midwest from 1854 to 1929 by recounting the story
of one boy and his brothers.
RNF ISBN 0-395-69822-7   PAP ISBN 0-395-91362-4
1. Lee Nailing. 2. Orphan trains—Juvenile literature. 3. Orphans—
United States—Biography—Juvenile literature. 4. Abandoned
children—United States—Biography—Juvenile literature. [1. Orphan trains.
2. Nailing, Lee; 1917–   3. Orphans. 4. Abandoned children.] I. Title.
HV985.W37   1996   362.7'34'092—dc20   [B] 94-43688 CIP AC

◆ ◆ ◆ ◆ ◆ ◆ ◆ ◆ ◆ ◆ ◆ ◆ ◆ ◆ ◆ ◆

FOR JAY, BECAUSE YOU BELIEVE,
AND FOR BEN, ALWAYS

◆◆◆◆◆◆◆◆◆◆◆◆◆◆◆◆ CONTENTS ◆◆

Orphan train riders ready to leave New York City and travel to Weatherford, Texas, in October 1912.

THE ORPHAN TRAINS

More than 200,000 children rode "orphan trains" in this country between 1854 and 1930. They were part of a "placing out" program created to find homes for children who were orphans or whose parents could not take care of them.

Most of the riders came from New York or other large cities in the East. The trains brought groups of them to other parts of the country where they were lined up in front of crowds of curious onlookers. Interested families could then choose the child they wanted. Within a week a child could go from living in an orphanage or on city streets to living in a Midwestern farmhouse or village. Many children found parents who loved them and took care of them; others never felt at home with their new families. Some were mistreated.

There is not much time left for orphan train riders to tell their stories. Those still alive are now elderly. Some will not talk about their experiences because they feel ashamed of being a "train kid" or because they did not find a happy home at the end of their ride. Others, like Lee Nailling, the man whose story is told in this book, believe that it is important for Americans to know about the orphan trains and the children who rode them.

CHAPTER ONE

LEE LOSES
HIS MOTHER

Lee Nailling was seven years old when his mother died. He cannot remember her and he does not remember her death. Lee's younger brother Leo, then four, remembers their mother's funeral and being lifted up by a neighbor so he could see her in her coffin. Lee cannot.

"I guess blocking everything out of my mind is how I got through it," Lee says. "The only photo I've ever seen of her showed her as a child. Her name was Julia. She was thirty-five when she died of complications after the birth of my youngest brother. I could see in that photo how beautiful she was. She had dark brown eyes and thick, wavy black hair."

In 1924, the year his mother died, Lee's name was Alton Lou Clement. He was the middle of seven children and had two older brothers, Ross and Fred, an older sister, Evelyn, and three younger brothers, Leo, Gerald, and George, the new baby. Another brother and sister had died as infants.

From what Lee can piece together about that time, his father was overcome with grief over his wife's death. For a few months he tried to care for his seven children. Then, perhaps because of his sorrow, or because he made too little money from their small farm in upstate New York, or because of some weakness in his own character, he gave up.

He told his three oldest children that they would have to leave home and take care of themselves. He gave the baby to family friends. Somebody else took Gerald, then a year old. Although he is now a great-grandfather, Lee has never forgotten what happened to Leo and himself:

"Someone—probably our father—took us to an orphanage and left us there: the Jefferson County Orphan Asylum in Watertown, New York. We had no idea what was happening to us. We just wanted to be with our family. Instead, we were suddenly in this strange, unfriendly place where no one ever spoke kindly to us. We slept in dormitories on cots surrounded by other kids. We were told we were orphans, but I didn't understand how we could be since our father was alive.

"At first Dad paid three dollars a week for our care. I guess that was too much for him because a short time later we became wards of the state. . . . We went from being part of a close family to feeling like outcasts. Nobody visited us, nobody wanted us, nobody loved us. We were just two more homeless kids in a country that already had too many."

Lee Nailling in 1993

TOO MANY ORPHANS

As a seven-year-old, Lee had no way of knowing that the care of large numbers of homeless and orphaned children had been a problem in America for almost a century. Before the 1800s, if children lost both parents, family members or neighbors would raise them. Usually the new parents did not legally adopt these children, but they might give them their family name and think of them as their own. The government rarely took part in these arrangements.

Even when orphanages became necessary, they were almost always run by charities like churches. Catholic nuns started the first American orphanage in 1729 in Natchez, Mississippi, for the children of settlers who had been killed by Indians. But for the next 100 years there were very few orphanages in this country.

By the early 1800s so many American children were orphaned or had a parent or parents who could not take care of them that the old system no longer worked. Huge orphanages were built, sometimes housing more than 1,000 children. Many of them were in big cities in the East, including Boston, Baltimore, Philadelphia, and New York. Others were in smaller places like Watertown.

Why were there so many orphans? Why could family and friends no longer take care of orphans as they had in the past? There are several reasons.

In the early 1800s the United States began to change from a country in which most people lived with several generations of their family on farms, to an industrial nation in which many people lived in cities where they knew no one. The invention of farm machinery meant that fewer workers were needed on farms. At the same time, thousands of workers were needed for the new factories being built in the cities. Too many people wanted the factory jobs, however, which kept wages low.

During the same period, hundreds of thousands of people came to the United States from other countries. These immigrants competed with farm workers for the factory jobs. There was not enough housing for everyone, and city landlords could charge high rents for places barely fit to live in. Many workers had large families and were jammed into tiny apartments that had to be shared with two or three other families. Some families even lived in cardboard boxes or in coal cellars.

The people lucky enough to find factory jobs often worked in dangerous conditions. If they were hurt or killed, other workers were always ready to take their place. People often worked 10 to 12 hours a day, 6 days a week. Even so, many parents could barely feed and clothe themselves and their children.

Children as young as five or six often labored long hours in factories to earn a few pennies a day. Others sold matches, shined shoes, peddled

This shoeshine boy lived in housing run by the Children's Aid Society.

newspapers, picked coal, or ran errands—anything to make a little money. Children barely old enough to walk begged in the streets.

Even when every member of a family worked, some families could not make enough money to survive. There was no welfare system. Some people starved to death. Others died from drinking too much alcohol or went insane. Sometimes parents were so upset at the birth of a child that they would abandon the newborn in a church or store, hoping someone

A family at work shelling peanuts in their apartment.

would find and care for the baby. Others did not even make that effort, and every day the police would find the bodies of infants who had been left to die in rain barrels and trash cans.

In other families the parents forced older children to leave to make space for a new baby, even if the children were only six or seven years old themselves. Homeless children slept on sidewalk heating grates, in doorways, or in empty buildings. They ate out of trash cans or stole food. Historians believe that in 1850, when New York City's population was 500,000, as many as 30,000 homeless children roamed the streets.

At that time the law treated children who were seven and older as adults, so the jails were often full of youngsters who had been caught stealing. Children of 12 and older could be put to death for that crime. Their punishment was carried out at public hangings that other street children would come to watch.

When charitable groups began to open orphanages in the cities, most of the children who lived in them came from the slums. A few orphanages were built outside of cities to care for the children of families like Lee Nailling's.

Children who lived in orphanages were called orphans, though about half, like Lee and Leo, had one or both parents still living. These parents either could not care for their children or had abandoned or abused them. Parents who were ill, fathers who were widowed, and mothers who were widowed or had never married sometimes put their children in orphanages because they had no way of taking care of them and no friends or relatives to help them. Some of these parents regularly visited their children and paid something for their care. If they could, they would eventually take their children home. Other children never saw their parents again.

Lee did not know if his father was going to come back for him and his brother. When the orphanage door closed, he felt like a prisoner who might never be freed.

CHAPTER THREE

LIFE IN THE ORPHANAGE

Seventy years later, Lee can still recall what life was like in the Jefferson County Orphan Asylum: "One of my chief memories is of hunger. Many nights I went to bed with my stomach growling. The food I remember eating the most was potatoes. We never got fresh vegetables or fruits. We never got a piece of candy. Both Leo and I were thin."

Lee still has a scar on his arm where another boy stabbed him with a fork when Lee reached for a biscuit. Hunger was also used as punishment. Children who misbehaved were denied a meal. That meant Lee often did not eat.

"My temper was a problem for me," Lee says. "I was always getting into fights. But even though I would have to miss a meal, I think my temper saved me. I struck back at the world with my fists when I was being put down. I refused to believe I was worthless."

Orphanage children attended the local town school and were often teased or bullied by other children there. If someone insulted Lee, saying that he needed a haircut, that his shirt had holes in it, or that he was no good "because you ain't got no mama," he would lash out. Lee was punished almost every day for fighting. He would be left alone in a tiny room for hours, made to drink bitter-tasting castor oil, or sent to bed without supper.

The adults in charge did not beat the children as they did at some orphanages, but they never showed the children any affection either. "They spoke to us very sternly," Lee says. "We were always being ordered around, told to stand here, to line up there. We had to march in line wherever we went. We lived off charity, wearing cast-off clothing people gave us. Our only gift at Christmas was an apple or orange. We had no future. It would have been easy to give in to hopelessness."

Lee did not give in. He cared for Leo the best he could and defended any smaller child who was being bullied. But he acquired a deep mistrust of adults. "What I learned was that all adults lied to you," he says. "Our father had deserted us; our other relatives didn't care about us; the people running the orphanage did only what they had to for us. I came to distrust anything an adult told me."

Though Lee often thought about running away, he stayed because Leo was too young to go with him, and there was no one else to watch out for him. Lee would lie awake at night wondering why no one came to visit them, and he vowed that as soon as possible, he would get himself and Leo out of the orphanage and find his brothers and sister.

Then one day in 1926, almost two years after their arrival at the orphanage, Lee, Leo, and some of the other children were told something amazing: They were going to ride a train!

"I had dreamed of being a train engineer," Lee says. "I'd seen trains puffing along in the distance and I'd always wanted to ride on one. I thought it would mean adventure, so I was real excited. What no one bothered to tell us kids was that the train was supposed to take us to find something I didn't want: a new family. That wasn't any ordinary train we were going to ride—it was an orphan train."

CHAPTER FOUR

THE FIRST
ORPHAN TRAINS

Orphan trains like the one Lee was about to board had been operating in the United States since 1854. By 1930, when they stopped running, the trains had carried about 200,000 homeless children from the city streets and orphanages of the East to new homes and families in the West, Midwest, and South.

The orphan trains were started by a minister named Charles Loring Brace. He had worked in the slums of New York City and was very worried about the homeless children. They needed housing, medical care, good food, warm clothing in winter, and schooling. In 1853, Brace started the Children's Aid Society. As soon as he opened an office in the slums, the children came. Brace wrote of them:

> Most touching of all was the crowd of wandering little
> ones who immediately found their way to the office.
> Ragged young girls who had nowhere to lay their heads;

Charles Loring Brace

children driven from drunkards' homes; orphans who slept where they could find a box or stairway; boys cast out by stepmothers or stepfathers; newsboys, whose incessant answer to our question "Where do you live?" rang in our ears, "Don't live nowhere!" little bootblacks, young peddlers . . . pickpockets and petty thieves trying to get honest work; child beggars and flower sellers growing up to enter courses of crime—all this motley throng of infantile misery and childish guilt passed through our doors, telling their simple stories of suffering, and loneliness, and temptation, until our hearts became sick.

Brace asked wealthy people to help support the Children's Aid Society. He also wrote articles and gave speeches for pay. He used all the money he raised to start programs to "help the children help themselves."

The Children's Aid Society opened centers where they served meals to needy children.

Boys learning to be blacksmiths at the Children's Aid Society's West Side Industrial Center in New York.

The homeless children needed somewhere to live, but Brace did not think orphanages were a good solution. Most were large, gloomy, over-crowded places that did not teach the children to become adults who could take care of themselves. That would happen, Brace believed, only if children had good families of their own. But where would the society find families to take so many needy children?

Brace thought he knew the answer: out West. To easterners like

Brace, "the West" was as far as the railroad could go. At that time it was the area of the country that today we call the Midwest and parts of the South. Like many people then, Brace had an idealized view of the West. He thought it was a place where there was plenty of food and all the people were goodhearted and generous. He was certain many would

People hoped that all the homeless city children could be taught to be useful members of society if they were raised in the country.

welcome another family member who could help with all the daily chores. He also believed westerners would accept the homeless children.

Brace created a plan he called "placing out." Trains would carry the children directly to areas where there were many farm and small-town families. The children would travel in groups or "companies." When they arrived in a town, people could gather and choose the child they wanted. A committee of respected citizens would judge if the families could give the children good homes.

Brace felt certain his plan could succeed—because it had before. He was not the first to think of moving homeless children who were born in one place to be raised by people in another. This had been done before with small numbers of children in England and Germany, as well as in the United States. By the time Brace's placing out program ended 75 years later, it had resulted in the largest children's migration in history.

Anxious to test his theories, in 1853 Brace sent 164 boys and 43 girls to homes in farming areas of New York and nearby states. These placements were a success. The young people found good homes and began learning trades.

Brace wasted no time. In 1854, the Children's Aid Society sent 46 boys and girls, ages 10 to 12, to a little town in Michigan. Within a week, every boy and girl had a home. Inspired by this success, the society made plans to send large groups of children west on what soon became known as orphan trains.

CHAPTER FIVE

THE PINK ENVELOPE

Lee remembers clearly what happened when he, Leo, and ten other children from the orphanage went to the train station to get on the orphan train:

"The girls had on new dresses, all alike, with white pinafores over them. We boys also had new clothes: knickers that buttoned below the knee, white dress shirts and neckties, and suit coats. I'd never had anything new before. All I'd ever worn was hand-me-downs from my older brothers or used clothes given to the orphanage. All of us felt real special. We wondered if we were going to meet the governor or something. We still had no idea what was actually happening."

He recalls how excited he felt while waiting for the train to arrive, with all the noise and confusion and people rushing around the station. As the train approached, its whistle blowing, the children began to clap their hands and jump up and down, but they were immediately hushed by the adults with them and told to line up and behave themselves because people were watching. As the children waited to climb up the big steps to the train, Lee kept his arm around Leo.

Then he heard someone call his name. Turning, he saw a man who was holding a little boy coming toward him. Leo did not know who the man was, but Lee let out a whoop of joy and ran into his father's arms.

"Dad told us that the little boy with him was our three-year-old brother, Gerald, who was going with us on the train. I didn't remember Gerald since he was only a year old the last time I saw him. When I asked my father where the train was taking us, he said to find a family who could care for us. How could this be? I insisted we wanted to be with him. I begged him to keep us, but he kept saying he couldn't.

"The other children were starting to board the train and we were holding up the line. My father thrust a long pink envelope into my hands. It had a stamp and an address on it. He said I was to keep my brothers with me and write to him when we got settled and let him know where we were. Before I could ask anything else, we were pulled from him."

Adults hurried Lee and his brothers onto the train, telling them to find their assigned seats in one of the two cars set aside for the children. Lee pushed away their hands, climbed onto a high velour seat, and pressed his face against the train window, trying to get one more look at his father. He could not see him anywhere—and would never see him again.

A group of orphan train riders and their sponsors pose for a picture before starting their trip.

"The matron who was going to take care of us on the train was a big-boned woman with a stern voice," Lee recalls. "She ordered me to come away from the window and get to my seat. I had to fight back the anger I felt. Then I touched the pink envelope in my coat pocket. At least I had that. As soon as I could, I would figure out how to get the three of us away from wherever it was we were being taken and I would find our father."

Even with so much to think about, Lee liked his first train ride. He was excited by the way the train swayed along, the wheels making a wonderful click-clacking noise on the tracks. Fields and small towns seemed to rush by. Lee had never had such a sense of freedom. He touched the pink envelope over and over, telling himself that everything was going to be all right.

He could hardly believe that Gerald was sitting between him and Leo. The little boy seemed to have no problem accepting his two big brothers and he snuggled against them. To this day Lee does not know where Gerald was between the time their mother died and the day their father gave him to Lee to take care of.

The food on orphan trains varied from trip to trip, but on Lee and his brothers' train, every meal was sandwiches, fruit, and milk. The boys gobbled up the first meal. They enjoyed it not only because it was different from what they were used to, but because there was enough of it.

The matron told Lee to take off his jacket so it would stay clean. He refused. When she insisted, Lee was not sure what to do. He had been taught to do what he was told. Finally he explained to her about the pink envelope and said he wanted to keep it next to him in his jacket's inner pocket. To his relief the matron left him alone.

The train stopped briefly at Grand Central Station in New York City, where 38 more orphans joined them, bringing the number of children in the two cars to 50. Lee knew it was 50 because everybody kept having to count off, saying their number out loud, until the matron was satisfied that every child was present. The train was soon out of the city and chugging westward through New Jersey.

The matron told the children that they were going west to find new homes, just as Lee's father had said. "This is an opportunity for you," she told them. "They call this an orphan train, and you're very lucky to be on it."

"I didn't believe her for a moment," Lee says. "In my mind this was just another trick adults were playing on kids. How could taking us away from the only things we'd ever known be an opportunity?"

He tried to understand what was happening. He was on an orphan train—a trainload of orphans. But that made no sense: "Leo and Gerald and I weren't orphans. We had a family, and I had the pink envelope to prove it. We didn't belong on any so-called orphan train. I was going to show them all. Somehow, some way, no matter where that train ended up, I'd get us back."

As soon as it was dark that first evening, the children began to get ready for bed. Lee helped Leo and Gerald stretch out on the seat and then carefully took off his jacket and laid it next to him. The pink envelope peeked out of the pocket just enough so that he could see it. He felt hopeful—a feeling he had almost forgotten. Their father had not abandoned them after all. He had come to the train. He had hugged them and wanted Lee to write to him. Lee thought about how surprised his father would be when the boys showed up on his doorstep. It would be wonderful! "I went to sleep with a smile on my face, happy for the first time since my mother had died," Lee says.

When he opened his eyes the next morning, the first thing he did was touch his jacket. It was right where he had put it. Then he reached into the pocket to touch the pink envelope. It was gone.

"I still remember the panic I felt," Lee says. "I pushed on Leo, making him wake up. We both began a frantic search all around the seat and on the floor. Nothing! I went through my jacket again, felt in the cracks between the seats and under the window. But there was no envelope."

Then he saw the matron standing over him. She sternly asked him what he was looking for. Lee begged her to help him find the envelope. She told him to sit down. When he started to protest, she said it louder. Lee sat. "Where you're going, you won't be needing that envelope," the matron said firmly. "You must forget about it."

"The truth struck me with blinding force," Lee remembers. "She had taken the envelope and there was nothing I could do about it. Absolutely nothing. Except hate her."

It was a bitter moment for him. "That pink envelope had given me back some hope. I can't explain how defeated I felt with it gone. It just took the life out of me. I wouldn't let anybody see me cry, but nights on that train I'd lie there with tears rolling down my cheeks and my heart breaking all over again. First my mother, then my other brothers and my sister, and now my father again. How could I have lost so much?"

CHAPTER SIX

FINDING HOMES FOR ORPHANS

Few of the children who climbed aboard orphan trains understood what was happening to them. Once they realized why they were taking the trip, their feelings differed. If they had been passed around from relative to relative, lived on the streets, been abused by their parents, or been in an orphanage, then they were likely to be pleased at the thought of finding a new family. Others, like Lee, did not want a new family and were angry to find themselves being taken to new homes.

In the early days of the trains, the Children's Aid Society sometimes took children off the streets or out of prison, but most of them came from orphanages. A few were signed over to the society by parents who wanted their children to have a chance for a better life than they could give them. Some children found their way to the society by themselves and asked to go on the trains.

Once a company of children was formed, they were bathed and given two sets of new clothes, including a hat, a coat, and shoes. Sometimes they were given a Bible. Many were taught manners—such as to eat neatly and say "thank you"—so that they would make a good impression on prospective parents. A number was pinned to their clothing to help the adults keep track of them during the trip.

Agents who worked for the Children's Aid Society looked for towns along the railroad tracks that were interested in having an orphan train stop there. Then they put up signs saying that a train was coming and set up the local screening committee—the people who would approve the families who wanted to choose a child.

Charles Loring Brace did not want families to adopt the children until it was clear that a child and a family were a good match for each other. That way the arrangement was not bound by law, and either the

---

TERMS ON WHICH BOYS ARE PLACED IN HOMES.

ALL APPLICANTS MUST BE ENDORSED BY THE COMMITTEE

Boys fifteen years old are expected to work till they are eighteen for their board and clothes. At the end of that time they are at liberty to make their own arrangements.

Boys between twelve and fifteen are expected to work for their board and clothes till they are eighteen, but must be sent to school a part of each year, after that it is expected that they receive wages.

Boys under twelve are expected to remain till they are eighteen, and must be treated by the applicants as one of their own children in matters of schooling, clothing and training.

Should a removal be necessary it can be arranged through the committee or by writing to the Agent.

The Society reserves the right of removing a boy at any time for just cause.

We desire to hear from every child twice a year.

All Expenses of Transportation are Paid by the Society.

CHILDREN'S AID SOCIETY.
24 ST. MARKS PLACE, N.Y.

E. TROTT, AGENT.

Poster explaining the terms for placing boys in homes.

child or the parents could end it if it was not a success. If that happened, the society would try to find the child another home. In fact, most of the early orphan train riders were never legally adopted, even if the child and family grew to love each other. Adoption was not common in the United States until the 1900s. Still, many of the children used their new family's name.

Sometimes children lived with several families before finding one they could stay with. Claretta Carman Miller of Colorado and her two sisters were neglected by their parents, so they were taken away from their home and put on an orphan train. Claretta was chosen by a family with nine children. They did not want another child—they wanted a servant.

A society agent tried to visit each child every year, but as the program grew bigger, that became difficult. Fortunately an agent visited Claretta after only two weeks and immediately took her away from the family. She endured bad treatment in two more homes before she arrived at the Carman farm late one rainy night. Mrs. Carman was a gentle, kind woman. It took her a year to nurse the sickly little girl back to health. With the Carmans, Claretta found loving parents and a real home at last.

If the birth parents were still alive, the society would try to get their written permission before sending a child west. But some parents did not understand what they were signing. When they tried to get their children back, the parents learned they were gone and could not be traced.

At first, the Children's Aid Society had only refused to give information to parents who had abused their children. Then the society stopped letting any parents know where their children were. Brace believed it was best for children to break with the past and start a new life, so once a child left on a train, neither parent nor child knew how to find each other.

Children were not allowed to bring any keepsakes with them, although some managed to smuggle a beloved photograph or locket on the journey west. Some older children did know how to reach their parents and stayed in touch with them. Others ran away and returned to their parents.

For most orphan train riders, who either did not remember their families or did not know how to find them, being denied information about themselves and their birth families often led to anger and frustration later in life. One rider was arrested as an adult for trying to steal his records. Some agencies would give basic facts like date and place of birth or copies of birth certificates; but few would reveal reasons why the parents had given up their children.

Arthur Field Smith of New Jersey, who rode an orphan train to Iowa in 1922, feels strongly that orphans should have access to any information that exists about them: "For medical and every other reason, orphans and their families have just as much right to know about themselves as those who are not orphans. There is stigma enough attached to being an orphan," he says.

Most placements were successful, and the program grew. During the first 20 years an average of 3,000 children rode the orphan trains each year. Brace continued to raise the needed money through his speeches and his writing. Railroads gave discount fares to the children, and wealthy people sometimes paid for whole trainloads of children.

Unfortunately, many children who needed homes were not allowed to go on the trains. It was always difficult to find homes for older children, and while some teenagers as old as 17 were successfully placed, 14 was usually the oldest a rider could be. It was always easiest to find homes for babies.

Children who were physically or mentally handicapped or sickly were usually left behind. So were children who had repeatedly committed crimes. They, too, would have been difficult to place. And almost all of the children who made the trip were white. The Midwest had been settled largely by white Europeans, mainly Germans, Scandinavians, English, and Irish. Most of the orphan train riders had those same backgrounds. The society knew that these children had the best chance of being chosen.

An advertisement in the Tecumseh, Nebraska, newspaper in 1893 announcing that an orphan train was coming to town listed children whom Brace felt would find homes. It read in part:

> All children received under the care of this Association are of SPECIAL PROMISE in intelligence and health, and are in age from one month to twelve years, and are sent FREE to those receiving them, on ninety days trial, UNLESS a special contract is otherwise made.
>
> Homes are wanted for the following children: 8 BOYS: Ages, 10, 6, and 4 years; English parents, blondes. Very promising, 2 years old, blonde, fine looking, healthy, American; has had his foot straightened. Walks now O.K. Six years old, dark hair and yes, good looking and intelligent, American. 10 BABES: Boys and girls from one month to three months. One boy baby, has fine head and face, black eyes and hair, fat and pretty; three months old.

From three or four to as many as 300 children went on one train for a trip that could last for a few days or a few weeks. Sometimes the children filled a whole car or even several cars. Older children cared for younger ones. Sometimes passengers and trainmen helped agents care for the children or gave money for food and milk. People also liked buying candy for them. At regular train stops, the children got off to play and run off energy.

Sometimes the children were lined up for people to see every time their train pulled into a station. Those not selected by townspeople got back on the train and went to the next town. But usually a company of children traveled to a specific place and children were not chosen along the way.

The success of Brace's orphan trains inspired several other groups to begin their own trains. Aside from the Children's Aid Society, the Foundling Hospital in New York City sent the largest number of children west.

The New York Foundling Hospital

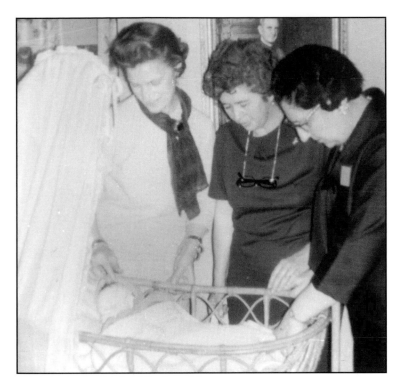

*Grown-up orphan
train riders from the
Foundling view the
cradle where mothers
left their babies in the
hospital's entryway.*

"Foundling" means an infant with unknown parents. The Foundling
was started in 1869 by Sister Irene of the Sisters of Charity to help New
York City's unwanted infants and small children. The day it opened, an
infant was abandoned on the front stoop. Others soon followed, and
Sister Irene put a wicker cradle in the entrance so babies could be left in
a safe place. So many babies were brought to the Foundling that in 1873
Sister Irene decided to start her own program to find homes for them.
Only Catholic families could apply. They sent the tiny children west on
what were sometimes called "baby trains." The new parents waited at the
depot to claim their assigned child, who would arrive wearing a tag with
the family's name on it.

One newspaper writer covering the story of a baby train's arrival interviewed a new father who said, "Beats the stork all hollow. We asked for a boy of 18 months with brown hair and blue eyes and the bill was filled to the last specification. The young rascal even has my name tacked on to him."

CHAPTER SEVEN

LEE ARRIVES IN TEXAS

As Lee's train continued its journey, his worrying increased. How would he ever find his way back to New York? What was going to happen to him and his brothers?

As always, whenever the train stopped so that the children could get some exercise, people gathered to watch. After a few days on the train, the matron told the children that there would be stops in several towns. In these towns, people would have the chance to select children. But none of the children was sure what this meant. Lee tried not to think about it.

The next day the train stopped at a town, and instead of being allowed to play, the children were marched to a church and seated on the stage. A crowd of people began to talk to them, touch them, and ask them questions. None of the children had written medical records, but, as the children quickly learned, people had their own ways of deciding if a child was healthy and strong.

Lee remembers a farmer in overalls coming up to him and feeling his muscles. Then the man stuck his hand in Lee's mouth to feel his teeth. Lee forced himself not to bite the man. When Lee glared at him, the farmer moved away.

That day Lee saw a small boy in the group being led away from his older brother. The little boy was screaming.

"I knew that all the family those boys had was each other," Lee says. "Just like my brothers and me. And I knew this was going to happen to us. The amazing thing was that it hadn't yet. We were healthy youngsters, and someone looking for workers was bound to pick one of us sooner or later. There didn't seem to be a thing in the world I could do to prevent it. I got back on the train that day with such a sense of dread that I felt like the world was going to end. As far as I was concerned, that might be the best thing that could happen."

Lee and his brothers had been on the train more than a week when it stopped in Clarksville, Texas. Of the 50 children who had started the trip, 25 had not yet been chosen by people in towns along the way. As much as Lee had liked the train in the beginning, he was tired of the swaying motion, the grim matron, and the same food. He was exhausted, dirty, and in need of a haircut.

He stepped from the train and looked around at a vast, empty horizon. The soil was reddish. There were few trees, and the late-winter air felt warm and dry. Texas was as different from upstate New York as Lee could have imagined.

As usual, a crowd was there to meet the train and walk with the children as they made their way to an old hotel on the main street of the little town. Everyone spoke with an unfamiliar accent, saying "y'all" and "howdy."

At the hotel, the children were told to sit on chairs lined up on the stage. Lee, Leo, and Gerald sat together. Just like before, people began to look them over.

Then a man and his wife stopped in front of Gerald. The woman spoke softly to Gerald and he smiled at her. When she opened her arms, he went right to her. Without a word to Lee and Leo, the couple walked away, holding Gerald. Lee wanted to run after them, to stop them, or to ask them to take him and Leo too. But he knew that the moment he stood up, he would be ordered to sit down.

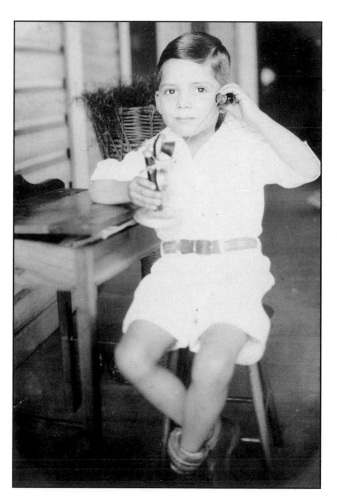

Lee's little brother Gerald was about five when this picture was taken.

He choked back tears while the couple signed papers in the back of the room. As they started to leave, Gerald realized what was happening and screamed out for Lee and Leo. Lee forced himself to try to block out the sound.

Then a gray-haired couple stood in front of Leo and began talking to him. Lee remembers thinking, "Now I'm going to lose Leo." And sure enough, the couple asked Leo if he would like to come home with them.

But this time something different happened. Leo gazed into the

Leo and his new family.

woman's kind face and said, "I want my brother to go too." Lee could hardly believe it when the man and woman looked at each other and nodded. They motioned both boys to go with them. The couple told the committee that their last name was Rodgers, and they had nine grown children. They had planned to take only one child, but were willing to try both boys.

Outside, Leo and Lee climbed into the Rodgers' model-T Ford. As they drove into the Texas countryside, Lee felt almost hopeful. Gerald was gone, but Lee would find him. No strangers were going to raise any of them. They *would* get back to New York. In the meantime, at least he and Leo were finally off the train and away from the matron. The brothers were together and this couple seemed nice. Lee hoped they would get good food to eat at the Rodgers' house. He was sick of sandwiches and fruit.

CHAPTER EIGHT

WHEN THE ORPHAN TRAINS CAME TO TOWN

When an orphan train puffed into town, almost everyone wanted to see the children. The viewing—sometimes called an open house or reception—was always packed. Even in towns of only a few hundred, more than 1,000 people might come to watch the children be chosen.

Sometimes the viewing was held right at the station, but usually the process was slower, with the children first going to the local hotel where they were fed, washed, and dressed in clean clothes. If there was time, they took naps before the viewing, which was held wherever there was a stage. This might be in a church, courthouse, school, opera house, or hotel.

Onlookers enjoyed the drama and excitement of watching people examine and choose the child they wanted, but the children were often terrified and confused. Most remember the experience as the worst part of being an orphan train rider. One rider later compared it to picking out puppies at the dog pound. At least one newspaper editor agreed, noting in an 1889 editorial that "the crowd standing around . . . were discussing [the children's] merits and demerits, like they would so many cattle they intended to purchase."

Others saw it differently. The editor of the *Hebron Journal* in Nebraska, writing in 1890 about the arrival of a trainload of children, observed that, "There was not a dull apathetic boy in the lot. All were bright and self reliant, and most of them had *good* faces. The greatest contest was for the possession of a sweet-faced, modest girl of fourteen. There were as many as a dozen wanted her."

How did people select a child? One journalist wrote,

It's a curious fact, but everybody who goes to pick out a child imagines that he or she is an advanced student of human nature, and no two persons have the same ideas on the subject. It is not a question of good looks so much as what they think of the child's disposition that influences the selection. "I want that boy because he has his hair combed," said one lady, pointing to a lad who stood to one side and took no part in his companions' conversation. "I'm sure he is a good little boy, and don't appear half so rough as the rest." She filled out the necessary papers and took the child away. The most mischievous boy in the crowd, a little brown-eyed, round-faced urchin, was picked out by a young couple from Carthage. "He will be able to do all the chores in a short time," said the young man as he led his charge out of the room.

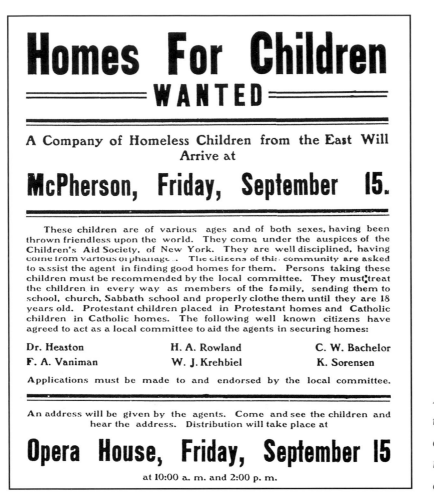

Homes For Children
═══ WANTED ═══

A Company of Homeless Children from the East Will Arrive at

McPherson, Friday, September 15.

These children are of various ages and of both sexes, having been thrown friendless upon the world. They come under the auspices of the Children's Aid Society, of New York. They are well disciplined, having come from various orphanages. The citizens of this community are asked to assist the agent in finding good homes for them. Persons taking these children must be recommended by the local committee. They must treat the children in every way as members of the family, sending them to school, church, Sabbath school and properly clothe them until they are 18 years old. Protestant children placed in Protestant homes and Catholic children in Catholic homes. The following well known citizens have agreed to act as a local committee to aid the agents in securing homes:

Dr. Heaston   H. A. Rowland   C. W. Bachelor
F. A. Vaniman   W. J. Krehbiel   K. Sorensen

Applications must be made to and endorsed by the local committee.

An address will be given by the agents. Come and see the children and hear the address. Distribution will take place at

Opera House, Friday, September 15
at 10:00 a. m. and 2:00 p. m.

Notices like this were handed out to announce the arrival of an orphan train.

Sometimes there were more interested families than available children. Other times there were more children than homes. If they could remain in town for a few days, children who had not been picked usually stayed with local families, and once in a while the families would decide to keep them. If no home was found, they rode to the next town or returned to New York or sometimes tried again on another train going west.

Bill Landkamer, who lives in Georgia, rode several orphan trains when he was a preschooler before finding a home in Nebraska. Bill does not know why, but as a small child he spoke only German. When he was finally chosen by the Landkamers, it may have been because Mr. Landkamer also spoke German.

Some local committees carefully chose each family, as Charles Loring Brace wanted them to, but others approved anyone who was interested. Willingness to take a child might be all that was asked of a family. Few committees tried to find out why a family wanted a child, how old the parents were, whether they were married or single, or how many other children they had.

Most agents tried to place brothers and sisters together or very near each other, but sometimes as many as seven brothers and sisters arrived together, making it impossible. Often even two siblings were separated.

Not all children got good homes. Some riders were physically or sexually abused, as some children are by their own parents. Some people just wanted help in the fields or in the house. The children who lived with them had to work very hard and were treated more like servants than family. Sometimes childless couples took children because they wanted someone to look after them in their old age or because they wanted someone to carry on the family name. Other riders were chosen to take the place of a child who had died. Some were even given the dead child's name.

That happened to August "Hoot" Gibson of Missouri, who lived in a Brooklyn orphanage until he was nine. He arrived in Kansas in 1923 and was taken by a family that changed his name to that of a son killed in World War I. Then he was placed with a different family, who gave him yet another name. When he joined the army during World War II, he took back the name he was born with.

Alice Bullis Ayler of Oklahoma never found a loving family. She spent much of her life pursuing one goal after another, trying to prove to herself that she was as good as anyone else. "I know I'm an overachiever—lots of orphan train riders are," she says. "We want to show the world that kids like us can succeed, too. It's tough because there was—and still is—so much bias against homeless children."

Alice Ayler (back row, left) was nine when this picture was taken. It is the last picture of the family before Alice's mother sent the children to the Children's Aid Society because she no longer wanted to care for them.

The excitement of selecting and bringing home a new son or daughter lasted a long time for some parents. Others wondered what had made them do something so foolish. Even when people had already agreed to take a child and had signed the papers, when they actually met their new son or daughter, they sometimes changed their minds. "I don't know what I was thinking of," said one woman, shaking her head. "I've already raised three boys and a girl, and that's enough." Several orphan train riders remember their assigned families refusing to take them because they did not look strong enough for hard work.

Riders who found loving families and stable homes still had problems. Some felt like outsiders all their lives. Others were teased about being a train kid or adopted or about somehow not being as good as other children.

Sometimes riders were so young when they made the trip west that they did not remember being adopted. If their families did not tell them, a schoolmate usually did. That is how Toni Weiler, who lives in Nebraska, found out. She had always known that her life with her parents was different from what she saw in other families. "We just never bonded," she says. "We weren't alike. I always felt sad and lonely when I was a child. My husband and I had eight children because I wanted a family more than anything in the world. I know I was trying to fill a void in my life."

Usually riders adjusted to their new lives, and they and their new families learned to love one another. When one girl wondered about her real mother, her adoptive mother always told her, "I wish I could have known her. She must have been a wonderful lady, because you are such a good girl."

Over and over again, for 76 years, orphan trains carried children to the Midwest and other parts of the country. People made their choices, sealing a child's fate. At the end of the viewing, after the paperwork was filled out, the children either got back on the train to try again or went home with strangers to begin their new lives.

The children climbing into buggies and wagons or early automobiles must have been filled with both excitement and fear. They finally had a family, but could not know what would happen next.

CHAPTER NINE

LEE FINDS A HOME

After a few days with Mr. and Mrs. Rodgers, Leo acted as though he had lived with them all his life. He called them Papa and Mama and became a favorite with their grown children. Lee hung back, not ready to trust any adult. He kept a careful eye on Leo. Unable to forget his experience at the orphanage, he ate his meals very fast so no one could take his food away.

By the end of the week he had begun to relax. He and Leo had spent hours exploring the farm, fishing in the pond, and chasing the chickens and hogs. Mrs. Rodgers had gotten both of them cleaned up, soaking them in the bathtub for a long time. She had washed their clothes and was talking about taking them into town for haircuts. Lee knew he needed one—his hair was so long it hung in his eyes.

When he heard a knock on the front door exactly one week after he had arrived, he thought nothing of it. "But when Mrs. Rodgers opened the door and the matron from the train came in, I panicked. What was she doing there? If there was one person on this earth I didn't want to see, it was that horrible woman who had stolen my pink envelope."

Mrs. Rodgers took Leo by the hand and told him to come with her. They left Lee alone with the matron. "All I remember her saying was, 'Get your things together. Mr. and Mrs. Rodgers have decided they can only keep one boy and they've settled on Leo. I've arranged for another couple to take you.'

"I told her I didn't want to go," says Lee, "but she said I had no choice in the matter. The next thing I knew I was in her car. She wasn't even going to let me say goodbye to Leo. But as the car started to pull away, Leo came around the corner of the house. He saw me with my face pressed to the window and he started to scream."

Lee watched helplessly as Leo ran after the car. The last thing Lee saw as the car left the farmyard was Mrs. Rodgers holding Leo and comforting him. By that evening, Lee had been left with an elderly farm couple who hardly seemed to know he was there. "I was as bitter as I could be," says Lee. "The only thing I was going to allow myself to think about was getting back to my father. It didn't matter how many places they took me."

During a dinner of greasy fried greens, no one said a word. Then the farmer told Lee to come along: It was time to bed down the hens and chicks. Lee followed the farmer to the chicken yard where he explained how the brood hens and their babies went into their wire cages at night for protection. During the day they walked around outside looking for food.

"I liked those little chicks," Lee remembers. "They were tiny and innocent and very soft to the touch. The old man didn't seem to mind when I picked them up and stroked them."

When Lee woke up the next morning he wanted to see the chicks.

He pulled on his clothes, sneaked out of the house, and went to the chicken yard. By the time he reached the wire cages, his shoes were soaked from the heavy dew. Since the farmer had said the chicks spent the day outside, Lee began pulling up the cage doors so the clucking hens and their babies could come out.

At breakfast he said nothing about the chicks. He followed the farmer out to the chicken yard when it was time to start chores, eager to show what he had done. But when they got to the cages, there in the dewy grass were the baby chicks—all dead!

The old man frowned at him. "Did you open the cages?" he asked angrily. "Don't you know them chicks drowned in the early dew? They wasn't to come out till the sun dried it up!" Lee was horrified that he had killed the fuzzy creatures. He had just been trying to help.

The farmer made Lee bury the chicks and would barely speak to him. The woman, as usual, was silent. Lee was miserable. When the farmer and his wife could not see him, he cried about what he had done. Late that afternoon, when the matron pulled up in her car and told him to get in, he did not even look back. He sat silent in the back seat as the car bounced over the rough Texas roads.

"I was really upset at what was happening to me," Lee recalls. "I felt terrible about killing the chicks, but I hadn't known any better. I didn't even care where I was being taken. I was nine years old and life stunk."

By the time the matron left him with another family, in the little village of Manchester, Texas, Lee had no hope that things would work out. He barely looked around at the large, comfortable house, nor would he smile at tall, friendly Ben Nailling. Ben's wife, Ollie, was short and plump and had kind eyes. She took Lee into her warm kitchen and gave him apples and milk, but he ate very little.

"I just wasn't hungry," he says. "I was willing to give them credit for at least acting interested in me, but the interest was all theirs. As far as I was concerned, the sooner I could get out of there, the better."

It was growing dark as they showed Lee around the grounds and the barns, and introduced him to the horses. Ben pointed to the woodpile and asked Lee to stack some wood for the kitchen stove on the back porch. Lee was immediately suspicious.

"I remembered that farmer who felt my muscles and teeth. It looked to me like the Naillings thought they'd found themselves a chore boy. I turned to him and said, 'Do it yourself. I didn't come here to work for you.' I think my voice was really angry because it sort of surprised me. They both looked shocked. Ben grabbed me by the arm and gave me a hard swat on the behind. He said, 'Now look here, boy, if you're going to be part of this family, you'll pull your weight. That stove has to be fed and that's to be your job and you don't ever talk to your elders like that. I think your disrespect went too far.'

"Well, that was too much for me. I refused to talk to either one of them. I figured I had nothing to lose because I wasn't going to be there in the morning, that was for sure. I meant to run away that very night."

Later that evening, Ollie showed him around his new bedroom. "Go to bed now and we'll get a fresh start in the morning," she said, smiling. Lee looked around in awe. He'd never had a room of his own before. Often he had shared his bed. But he still was suspicious. "I decided it was just a trick to soften me up before they put me to work, and I was determined I wouldn't fall for it."

*Ben, Lee, and
Ollie Nailling*

He climbed onto the big feather bed and sank down into its softness. Ollie came back and sat by him. She said she knew he was tired and she hoped he would sleep well. Then she tucked the covers around him and gave him a kiss on the cheek before she left the room.

"I couldn't remember the last time anyone had kissed me," Lee says. "It rekindled a memory in me—maybe of my mother. I started to cry and I buried my head in the pillow so they wouldn't hear me. I think I cried half the night."

The next morning, he awoke to Ben shaking him and telling him to get up for breakfast. His bedroom was flooded with sunshine.

"I was so surprised that it was already morning," Lee says. "I had planned to sneak out after the house was quiet. But I felt better after a good night's sleep and figured I could run away the next night. I got dressed and went to the kitchen, following my nose to all these delicious smells."

Ollie greeted him and told him they were going to eat in the dining room. "We only eat there on special occasions," she said. The table was heaped with ham, bacon, eggs, grits, biscuits, potatoes, jams, and jellies. Lee thought company must be coming, but saw only three place settings. After Ben motioned for him to sit, Lee immediately grabbed a biscuit and started to take a bite out of it, but Ollie stopped him. "We say grace first," she said, telling him to bow his head and close his eyes.

"I did what she told me, but I was wishing she would hurry up so I could eat. That food smelled so good," Lee says.

"Then I started to listen to her. She was thanking God out loud for the beautiful day and the recovered health of a friend who had been sick, and for the bounty of food we were about to enjoy. Then she said an amazing thing: 'Father, thank you for sending our new son to us, for the privilege of allowing us to raise him. We will try to be good parents to him.'

"I'm sure my jaw dropped in amazement. Somebody was actually thankful I was there? I had always felt like a bother to adults, but this woman was acting like she was glad I was there! I stole a glance at Ben. He smiled at me and said, 'We're happy you're with us, son. Now let's eat.'"

Lee stuffed himself. He could not remember when food had tasted so good. The more he ate, the more pleased the Naillings seemed to be.

Ollie and Ben Nailling

After breakfast they said they would take him to the store they owned to get him some new clothes, and then to the barbershop for that much-needed haircut.

Lee clearly remembers the walk down the lane into the village, Ben and Ollie on either side of him. They stopped at each of the six houses along the way, and at each one they introduced Lee as "our new son" and said how glad they were that he was with them. By the time Lee was fitted for new clothes and had his hair cut, he already knew some of the villagers by name and had met several children his own age.

By the end of the day, after another home-cooked meal, he had decided to give the new arrangement a chance, at least for a little while. The Naillings' house was beginning to feel like home.

CHAPTER TEN

THE LAST ORPHAN TRAINS

A 1910 Children's Aid Society report said that 87 percent of the orphan train riders had "done well." We cannot know exactly what the society meant by that, but 87 percent is a high success rate, especially since so many of the children had troubled beginnings. The riders have included a governor of a state, a governor of a territory, two members of Congress, two district attorneys, a justice of the Supreme Court, sheriffs, mayors, judges, college professors, clergymen, school superintendents, bankers, lawyers, postmasters, teachers, engineers, and at least 7,000 soldiers and sailors.

Several were famous. Orphan train rider Andrew Burke was a drummer boy in the Civil War. He became a newspaperman and then governor of North Dakota from 1870 to 1873. Burke expressed his appreciation for the program and urged homeless children to join it.

John Green Brady was on the same orphan train as Andrew Burke.

No one would have guessed that Brady would amount to much. His mother had died when he was seven. He ran away from home because his father would get drunk and beat him. Then the police put Brady in an orphanage, and he rode an orphan train to Indiana. There a judge named John Green took him because "I considered him the homeliest, toughest, most unpromising boy in the whole lot. I had a curious desire to see what could be made of such a specimen of humanity."

Eventually Brady graduated from Yale University and Union Theological Seminary. He became a missionary, went to Alaska, set up the Indian Industrial School in Sitka, and was named territorial governor of Alaska in 1897.

Henry Lee Jost rode an orphan train to Missouri. As an adult he earned his law degree and in 1912 became mayor of Kansas City, Missouri. Known as the Orphan Boy Mayor, he served until 1916.

Thousands of other orphan train riders have made their mark in other ways. As a group they are generous to charities, have a low divorce rate, and are devoted to their families. Many of them have foster children or adopted children, according to Mary Ellen Johnson, executive director of the Orphan Train Heritage Society of America (OTHSA).

Johnson says that about 500 known orphan train riders were still living in 1996. All were 70 or older. She estimates that 2 million people are the descendants of orphan train riders.

"I feel the riders are a tribute to Charles Loring Brace and his vision," she says. "The placing out program . . . proved that putting orphaned or abandoned children in institutions didn't have to be the only option to leaving them on the streets or with unfit parents. Brace proved that families would take the children in and give them homes. Even if they were required to work hard for their new families, the children's chances of growing to adulthood and becoming productive citizens were much better than if they had stayed where they were."

The program ended in 1930 because of new laws and a variety of new programs designed to help children and immigrants.

Some of the laws limited how many hours children were allowed to work. Other laws controlled adoption and kept people from "importing" children. These laws made it difficult—and in some states impossible—to bring in trainloads of orphans.

The number of immigrants coming into the country each year lessened. New programs helped immigrants find jobs and housing, helping to prevent the poverty that had led some earlier immigrants to abandon their children. At the same time, the government began the welfare program, offering monthly payments to poor families. Other new programs helped keep troubled families together.

Large orphanages became a thing of the past. They were replaced by individual and small-group foster homes. Today the Children's Aid Society and other groups continue their work to improve the quality of the lives of poor children in New York City and many other places.

CHAPTER ELEVEN

LEE LOSES ONE BROTHER AND FINDS TWO MORE

Ben and Ollie Nailling were patient people. They were willing to give Lee all the time he needed to settle in and feel at home. After a few fights at school, which earned him the respect of the other boys, Lee started to make friends. Soon he had the run of the village and plenty of playmates. The Naillings gave him a pony and let him keep the dog that followed him home one day.

Gradually he turned into a Texan. "I got teased a lot because of my New York accent," Lee recalls. "I would be saying 'youse guys' while everyone around me was saying 'y'all' in a strong Texas accent. I picked up the Texas way pretty quickly."

Along with a new accent, new friends, and new pets, he got a new name. When he was born in 1917 his parents named him Alton Lou Clement, and he had always been called "Al" or "Alton." Ollie Nailling strongly disliked a New York politician named Al Smith. No son of hers—particularly a son who came from New York—would be called Al. Ollie thought Lee's middle name was "Lee" rather than "Lou," so she asked her new son if they could name him "Lee Clement Nailling." Lee agreed, and that is the name on his adoption papers.

After a while, Lee got over his desire to run away. The Naillings made sure he saw his brothers as often as possible. The three families arranged for the brothers to spend part of each summer together, first at one house and then the next. They did that until the brothers grew up.

"I didn't want to admit it, but I liked my new home," Lee says. "As for my new parents, well, they took me to their hearts. In their eyes I was their son. They'd never had children and I think they really did consider me a blessing from God."

But sometimes Lee would think about what had happened to him, and the old bitterness would return. If Ben or Ollie tried to talk to him about his past, he would become silent.

"For years I felt like something was missing in my life." Lee says.

"I had a wonderful family in the Naillings, but I often wondered about my biological family. Leo didn't seem troubled by it, and Gerald was so young that he didn't remember anything about New York. Not me. The lost pink envelope worried me for years and years. I often dreamed of finding my family. I thought I'd look up one day and see my biological father coming toward me to take me home. That thought never left me.

"But even though I was still angry at the whole world for what had happened to me, I couldn't hold out forever. My new parents gradually wore me down. I not only learned to love them deeply and to call them

Lee and his grand-mother, Ollie Nailling's mother.

From left to right: Lee with a family friend and his adoptive father.

Mom and Dad and mean it, but I also gained a wonderful grandmother and an assortment of aunts, uncles, and cousins. The little town of Manchester turned out to be the best place in the world to grow up."

When Lee arrived at the Naillings' house in 1926, he was scared, bitter, and grieving for his family. He thought all adults were untrustworthy. Over the next few years he became outgoing and friendly, good at his schoolwork and at sports. He stayed in close touch with Gerald and Leo. He grew up working hard in his parents' store and on the farm. His father also owned the local gristmill, and every Saturday Lee helped with the hard job of grinding corn into meal by running the heavy grinding machine.

He loved his adoptive mother for her kind heart, her strong religious beliefs, her talent for cooking, and her loyalty to her family. He loved his adoptive father for his sense of fair play and justice and his determination to raise Lee well.

After Lee graduated from high school, he went to business college in Dallas. While living in Dallas, he fell in love with a young woman named Novelle. They were married in 1939, and a year later their daughter, Jere Lee, was born.

By 1944 Ben Nailling had died and Lee was helping Ollie run the family business. Novelle was pregnant with their second child. But World War II was raging throughout Europe and the South Pacific, and Lee was drafted into the army. Gerald, who had grown up tall, handsome, and good natured, had volunteered for the army several years earlier and was stationed in the Philippines. Leo had also joined up and asked to be sent

Lee and Novelle the year they met

to the South Pacific in order to be near Gerald. Then came terrible news: Gerald had been taken prisoner by the Japanese. Lee was in military training at the time and he and Novelle were getting to know their new son, Lee Nailling, Jr. More bad news came: Lee was being sent to Europe.

"Having to go overseas when all I wanted was to be with my family was sure tough," Lee says. "It was too much like what had happened to me as a child. Once again I had no control over my life. This time I felt like I was a prisoner of the government."

In 1945, just as the defeat of Germany was certain, Lee was assigned to help guard a German prisoner-of-war camp. It troubled him that he was guarding German prisoners while his brother Gerald was a prisoner of the Japanese. Lee knew how hard the lives of war prisoners were. "I was afraid every day for him," Lee says.

While Lee was still in Germany, the family received word of a tragedy. Gerald had been on a Japanese prison ship when it was sunk by sailors on an American submarine who did not know that American prisoners were on board. The little brother whom Lee had cared for on the orphan train was dead.

Lee returned from World War II unharmed, but grieving for Gerald. He became a food store manager, and he and Novelle devoted themselves to their children. They also took care of Ollie Nailling in the years before her death. The family settled in Atlanta, Texas, a town of 6,000 near the village where Lee had grown up. He was active in the church and local organizations and was honored by the chamber of commerce as Man of the Year for the many ways he had helped his town.

After Lee retired, he and Novelle remained involved in volunteer groups, visited back and forth with Leo and his family, and enjoyed their grandchildren and great-grandchildren. Their daughter, Jere Lee, married J. R. Lummus. Lee Nailling, Jr., married Jeanie Warren, and they became the parents of Brian, Teresa, and David. Brian and his wife, Dawn, now have a son named Christopher. Teresa, inspired by her grandfather's story, adopted a little boy named Joshua. Then in 1984, when Lee was 67 and thought life could not hold any more surprises for him, he got one of the greatest of all.

After a story about him appeared in the newspaper, Lee received a letter from a man who had been friends with his older brother Fred. The man said that Fred had recently died but that Lee's oldest brother, Ross, was in Florida. Included in the letter was a phone number.

Lee immediately dialed the number. In his Texas accent he asked if he was speaking to the Ross Clement who used to live near Watertown,

New York. He was. The voice with the New York accent belonged to his big brother.

Ross told Lee that both he and his sister, Evelyn, had tried to find him, Leo, and Gerald. At different times they had gone to the Children's Aid Society, only to be told that the children had been sent far away and there was no way to trace them. Ross said that Evelyn was dead too. After the family split up, he and Fred had grown up together on the streets. Fred had not had children, but he had taken great pleasure in paying for summer outings for several orphans every year.

"We used to run into our father once in a while, but he barely acknowledged us," Ross told Lee. "He was a broken, bitter man when he died, and as far as we know, he died alone. I have to tell you, Lee, I just think he was no good. Otherwise, he wouldn't have given up all us kids."

Lee was not ready to agree with that: "That day he gave me the pink envelope, Leo remembers that Dad was crying. I think he really cared about us. I often wonder how it would have changed things if I hadn't lost that envelope."

Ross said that George—the baby brother who had been taken by family friends after the death of their mother—still lived in New York. Then Lee told Ross about Leo, and he had to tell Ross that Gerald had died in the war.

Of the original family, Evelyn, Fred, and Gerald were dead. But Ross, Lee, Leo, and George were alive, and they wanted to get to know each other. Lee and Novelle's children, Jere Lee and Lee, Jr., organized a reunion. People heard about it—many of them learning about orphan trains for the first time—and the chamber of commerce planned a party for the brothers.

From left to right: George, Ross, Leo, and Lee in 1984

On Memorial Day, 1984, a car pulled up to the Nailling home. Lee stood by the window watching it. He had been unable to sleep the night before because he was so excited. "I'm not sure I can explain my emotions," he says. "I wondered if Ross and I would feel any kind of bond, if we would know we were family. I guess what worried me was that there wouldn't be any feeling between us."

He saw a small man with wavy white hair get out of the car, and then he ran out the door and down the walk to throw his arms around the brother he had not seen in 60 years. "It was wonderful," Lee says. "No one can imagine the feeling. This was my brother and I loved him. The moment of knowing that is frozen in time for me."

George and Leo and their families soon arrived, and the brothers spent the weekend getting to know each other. "Those were some of the happiest days of my life," Lee remembers. "Ross died a few years ago and I'm very grateful I had some time with him. I feel so lucky to have found him. George and I are in regular touch, and I often see Leo since he lives nearby."

Lee frequently speaks to school children about his experiences as an orphan train rider. He shows children the scar on his arm where the boy at the orphanage stabbed him with a fork as he reached for a biscuit. He tells them about the pink envelope and about being separated from Gerald and then being taken away from Leo when they got to Texas. He tells them about the dead chicks. Sometimes when he has finished speaking, children will come up to him to talk about problems in their lives— fathers who don't live with them or mothers who drink or money troubles that keep their families moving around.

Lee tells them that their attitude toward what happens to them is the key to their lives. "I was bitter for a long time," he says to them. "I let that bitterness eat at me and it wasn't good for me. I was fortunate to get loving parents who were able to help me put away the bad things that had happened to me so I could focus on the good. But I have met many orphan train riders who had terrible things happen to them and who didn't get good families, and on their own they determined to have good lives and have done that. You can too."

In 1994 Lee received an award named for Charles Loring Brace from the Orphan Train Heritage Society. It is given each year to a rider who has helped people learn about the orphan trains. Lee is proud of the award. He believes that Americans should know about the orphan trains and their role in history.

When Lee looks back on his life, he believes himself to be one of the luckiest orphan train riders. "I've always felt that I had a guardian angel watching over me," he says. "When I got off that train in Texas, I was a bitterly unhappy little boy with a heart full of grief. The good Lord saw to it that I ended up with the Naillings. That was where I belonged."

POSTSCRIPT

The fall of 1996, Lee, Novelle, and their daughter, Jere, were with me in New Hampshire when I received the prestigious Boston Globe–Horn Book Award for this book. At the award ceremony, 400 librarians gave Lee a standing ovation. I assure you, there wasn't a dry eye in the house.

Lee was aglow at the ceremony. He had just visited the old orphanage in Watertown, New York, where he was received as an honored guest (today it's a model home for troubled children). He saw his and Leo's names in the ancient ledger book. He also met two first cousins and received a copy of his family tree. Best of all, he learned where his mother was buried and was able to visit her grave. He said he felt so peaceful there, as if he'd traveled full circle. "Now I know where I come from, I know where I am, and I know how I got here," he said, "and I'm as thankful as I can be."

In March 2001, Lee died. He was 83 years old and had been ill with cancer. Both Novelle and Leo had died the previous year, and it just wasn't the same for Lee once they were gone. His children and grandchildren were with him until the end.

Like his family, I miss him very much. He was a gentle soul, and a giving soul. He had a kind word and a warm smile for everyone. The world was a brighter place when he was in it.

RECOMMENDED BOOKS, VIDEOS, AND WEB SITES

We Rode the Orphan Trains (Houghton Mifflin) by Andrea Warren. The true stories of eight riders and one of the agents who rode west with the children.

The Orphan Train series (Bantam Books) by Joan Lowery Nixon. Each book features a different fictional character who rode an orphan train. For middle grade readers.

Train to Somewhere (Clarion Books) by Eve Bunting. Fictional story about a little girl on an orphan train who is looking for a home. Appropriate for early elementary readers.

"Orphan Trains," a documentary produced for *American Experience* on PBS. Includes interviews with several orphan train riders, including Lee Nailling.

AndreaWarren.com. The author's Web site includes excerpts from her books and historical information about the orphan trains.

Orphantrainriders.com. The official Web site of the Orphan Train Heritage Society of America includes history, interviews with riders, and ordering information for books and other items of interest related to the orphan trains.

cc.ukans.edu/carrie/kancoll/articles/orphans/. This site features information and links about the orphan trains and their riders, especially those who rodc to Kansas.

pbs.org/wgbh/amex/orphan/index.html. Public television has included background information and the script for the production "Orphan Trains," a documentary that appeared on the program *American Experience*.

The Orphan Train Heritage Society of America, a nonprofit volunteer organization, will send a packet of materials to interested students and educators. To receive, send two first-class stamps to: OTHSA, 614 East Emma Avenue, Suite 115, Springdale, Arkansas 72764-4634. Phone: 479-756-2780. E-mail: othsa@msn.com.

BIBLIOGRAPHY

The Children's Aid Society of New York: Its Emigration or Placing Out System and Its Results. New York: The Children's Aid Society, 1910.

Fry, Annette Riley. "The Children's Migration." *American Heritage Magazine*, December 1974, 4–10.

Holt, Marilyn Irvin. *The Orphan Trains*. Lincoln: University of Nebraska Press, 1992.

Jackson, Donald Dale. "It Took Trains to Put Street Kids on the Right Track Out of the Slums." *Smithsonian*, August 1986, 95–103.

Johnson, Mary Ellen, and Kay B. Hall, eds. *Orphan Train Riders: Their Own Stories*, volumes 1 & 2. Baltimore: Gateway Press, 1922, 1993.

Patrick, Michael, Evelyn Sheets, and Evelyn Trickel. *We Are a Part of*

History. Santa Fe, NM: Lightning Tree Press, 1990.

Wheeler, Leslie. "The Orphan Trains." *American History Illustrated,* December 1983, 10–23.

ACKNOWLEGMENTS

I will always be grateful to Lee and Novelle Nailling for their assistance, patience, and interest during the writing of this book. Their daughter, Jere Lummus, helped in various ways. Also, my thanks to my agent, Regina Ryan; my editors, Norma Jean Sawicki, Judy Levin, and Audrey Bryant; Mary Ellen Johnson and the Orphan Train Heritage Society of America; and the many orphan train riders who told me their stories. I am especially grateful to rider Alice Bullis Ayler, one of the bravest women I know.

Thanks to the following for assistance with photos and information: the Adams County Historical Society, Hastings, Nebraska; Victor Remer of the Children's Aid Society; the New York City Foundling Hospital; the Lawrence, Kansas, Public Library; the New York Historical Society; the Museum of the City of New York; and the Orphan Train Heritage Society of America.

Page numbers in **boldface** type refer to illustrations.